EXPLORING BIOMES

TUNDRA BIOMES

by Lela Nargi

pogo

Ideas for Parents and Teachers

Pogo Books let children practice reading informational text while introducing them to nonfiction features such as headings, labels, sidebars, maps, and diagrams, as well as a table of contents, glossary, and index.

Carefully leveled text with a strong photo match offers early fluent readers the support they need to succeed.

Before Reading

- "Walk" through the book and point out the various nonfiction features. Ask the student what purpose each feature serves.
- Look at the glossary together. Read and discuss the words.

Read the Book

- Have the child read the book independently.
- Invite him or her to list questions that arise from reading.

After Reading

- Discuss the child's questions. Talk about how he or she might find answers to those questions.
- Prompt the child to think more. Ask: Why do few trees grow in the tundra biome?

Pogo Books are published by Jump!
5357 Penn Avenue South
Minneapolis, MN 55419
www.jumplibrary.com

Library of Congress Cataloging-in-Publication Data

Names: Nargi, Lela, author.
Title: Tundra biomes / by Lela Nargi.
Description: Minneapolis, MN: Jump!, Inc., [2023]
Series: Exploring biomes | Includes index.
Audience: Ages 7-10
Identifiers: LCCN 2022000116 (print)
LCCN 2022000117 (ebook)
ISBN 9781636907659 (hardcover)
ISBN 9781636907666 (paperback)
ISBN 9781636907673 (ebook)
Subjects: LCSH: Tundra ecology—Juvenile literature.
Classification: LCC QH541.5.T8 N37 2023 (print)
LCC QH541.5.T8 (ebook)
DDC 577.5/86—dc23/eng/20220104
LC record available at
https://lccn.loc.gov/2022000116
LC ebook record available at
https://lccn.loc.gov/2022000117

Editor: Eliza Leahy
Designer: Emma Bersie

Photo Credits: Gregory A. Pozhvanov/Shutterstock, cover (left); Rtstudio/Shutterstock, cover (right); Pi-Lens/Shutterstock, 1; meunierd/Shutterstock, 3; Troutnut/Shutterstock, 4; MoLarjung/Shutterstock, 5; Vadim Nefedov/Alamy, 6-7; Arterra Picture Library/Alamy, 8-9; Viktor Loki/Shutterstock, 10; Justas in the wilderness/Shutterstock, 11; Marayapiraya/Dreamstime, 12-13t; blickwinkel/Alamy, 12-13b; BGSmith/Shutterstock, 14-15tl; Vaclav Sebek/Shutterstock, 14-15tr; Jukka Jantunen/Shutterstock, 14-15bl, 16-17tr; Agami Photo Agency/Shutterstock, 14-15br; moosehenderson/Shutterstock, 16-17tl; Michael Benard/Shutterstock, 16-17bl; Tom Tietz/Shutterstock, 16-17br; Cenk Unver/Dreamstime, 18; ARCTIC IMAGES/Alamy, 19; Abaca Press/Alamy, 20-21; Alexey Seafarer/Shutterstock, 23.

Printed in the United States of America at Corporate Graphics in North Mankato, Minnesota.

TABLE OF CONTENTS

CHAPTER 1

COLD AND WINDY

Which of Earth's **biomes** is the coldest and windiest? Welcome to the tundra! Little can survive –40 degree Fahrenheit (–40 degree Celsius) temperatures. *Brr!*

There are two kinds of tundra. Alpine tundra is on mountaintops. These areas are more than 10,000 feet (3,048 meters) high. The Himalayas in Asia are one example.

Arctic tundra is in the far north. It covers parts of Antarctica, too. Summers are shorter than in alpine tundra. Winters are colder and longer. They last 10 months or more.

TAKE A LOOK!

Tundra makes up about 20 percent of Earth's land. Take a look!

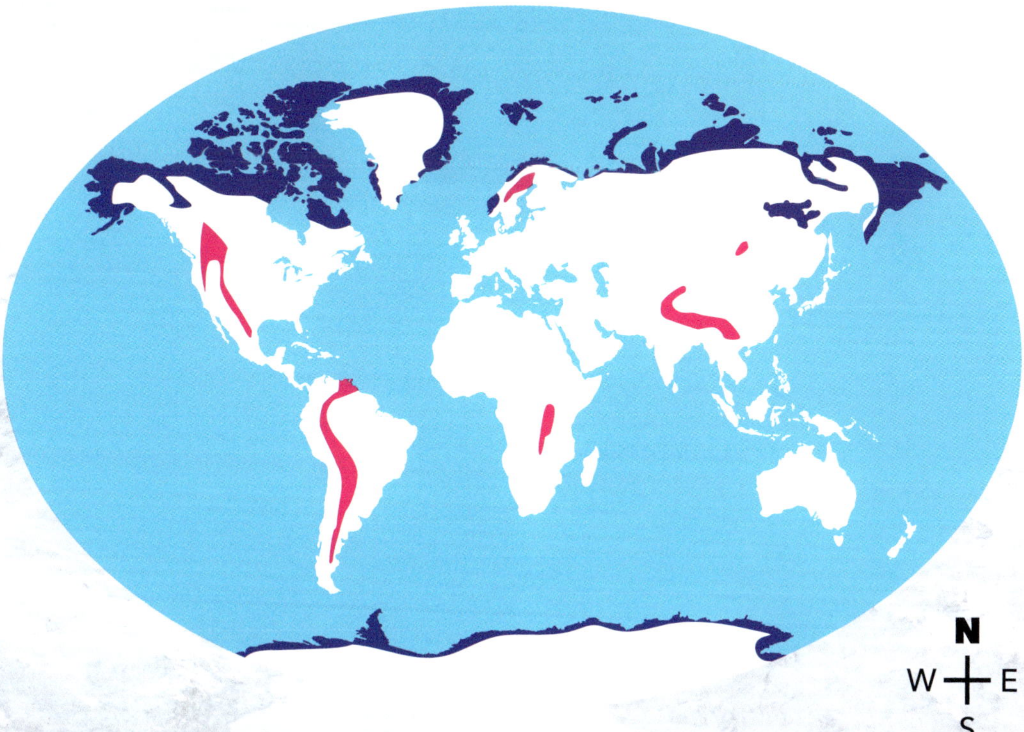

■ = alpine tundra ■ = Arctic tundra

The tundra is dry. It gets about 10 inches (25 centimeters) of **precipitation** each year.

You might find a birch or willow tree. But few trees can grow in the tundra. Why? They need **moisture**. It is also hard for their roots to grow in **permafrost**.

DID YOU KNOW?

Trees block wind. Since the tundra has few trees, winds are strong.

birch
tree

CHAPTER 2

LIFE IN THE TUNDRA

Life is hard in the tundra. Fewer kinds of plants and animals live here than in any other biome. Plants only grow during the short summers. Many have dark leaves. Bearberry has red leaves! The dark color soaks up more sunlight.

Many plants have thick leaves. This helps them hold moisture. Plants grow close to each other for warmth. Pasqueflower stems are hairy. This protects them from wind. It helps them stay warm.

Summer is a busy time in the tundra. There are 400 kinds of tundra flowers. Many have bright petals. This helps bees find them. Arctic bumblebees sit in flowers to get warm. This shields them from wind.

Alpine animals like lemmings eat a lot during summer. They raise their young while there is a lot of food.

DID YOU KNOW?

Arctic bumblebees shiver to get warm. Their large size also helps them stay warm.

Arctic
bumblebee

lemming

bighorn sheep

polar bear

Arctic hare

Arctic fox

Animals **adapt** to survive the cold winter. In alpine tundra, bighorn sheep grow thicker coats. Layers of fur keep polar bears warm in the Arctic tundra.

Some animals' fur turns white. It blends in with snow. This helps Arctic hares hide from **predators**. It helps Arctic foxes hunt.

Pikas hide under rocks in winter. They store hay. They eat it until spring. Some animals, like Arctic squirrels, **hibernate**. Wood frogs also hibernate. Their bodies freeze. Then they **thaw** in summer!

Other animals **migrate**. Why? There is not much to eat in winter. Caribou travel south. They find food there.

pika

Arctic squirrels

wood frog

caribou

CHAPTER 3

THE TUNDRA AND US

The tundra has been home to humans for around 45,000 years. Many people still live here. Some Sami people raise reindeer in Finland!

Scientists study **volcanoes** in the tundra. They study wildlife. They dress very warm!

In the tundra, dead plants and animals can stay frozen for thousands of years. Scientists have found the **remains** of **extinct** animals, such as woolly mammoths, in tundra ice. We can see them in museums. They help us learn how life **evolved** on Earth.

What else do you think we can learn from the tundra?

DID YOU KNOW?

Scientists study **climate change** in the tundra. Ice is melting. Permafrost is thawing. This makes it harder for plants, animals, and people to survive.

woolly mammoth remains

ACTIVITIES & TOOLS

TRY THIS!

WARM LAYERS

Tundra animals need to keep warm in the cold. Just one layer of fur won't cut it! See how layers keep animals warmer in this fun activity.

What You Need:

- large bowl
- cold water
- ice cubes
- one pair of cotton gloves
- one pair of leather or latex gloves
- clock or watch

1. **Fill a large bowl with cold water.**
2. **Add ice cubes and stir until the water is very cold.**
3. **Put a cotton glove on each hand. On one hand, put a leather or latex glove over the cotton glove.**
4. **Have a clock or watch nearby. Hold your hands under the water for two minutes. Which hand is colder? Why do you think this is? How do you think extra layers help keep tundra animals warm?**